Soup Cookbook

Simple and Nutritious Homemade Soups for a Better Body and a Healthier You

Copyright © 2020

All rights reserved.

DEDICATION

The author and publisher have provided this e-book to you for your personal use only. You may not make this e-book publicly available in any way. Copyright infringement is against the law. If you believe the copy of this e-book you are reading infringes on the author's copyright, please notify the publisher at: https://us.macmillan.com/piracy

Contents

Thai Chicken Soup 1

Detox Chicken Soup 4

Mediterranean Kale, Cannellini And Farro Stew 7

Jalapeño Lime Chicken Soup 10

Cabbage Soup 13

Pesto Chicken Minestrone 16

Savory Pumpkin Soup With Spice Shake 19

Crock Pot Chicken Tortilla Soup 22

Chicken Vegetable Soup 25

Lemon Chicken And Cauliflower Rice Soup 28

Vegetable Beef Soup 31

30 Minute Pesto Chicken, Kale + White Bean Soup 34

Lentil Soup 37

Curried Cauliflower Soup 40

Superfood Quinoa Soup 43

Paleo Turkey Meatball Zoodle Soup 46

15 Minute Tomato Basil Soup With Pesto 50

Italian Wedding Soup 53

Spinach And White Bean Soup 56

Summer Vegetable, Chicken, and Gnocchi Soup 59

Snap Pea-and-Lettuce Soup 61

Thai Chicken Soup

yield: 4 SERVINGS

prep time: 15 MINUTES

cook time: 20 MINUTES

total time: 35 MINUTES

INGREDIENTS

2 teaspoons oil, I used coconut oil

1 red bell pepper, chopped

1/2 cup minced shallots

8 ounces sliced mushrooms

1 stalk lemon grass, cut in half lengthwise

1 tablespoon fresh grated ginger

3 cloves of garlic, grated or minced

1 cup snow peas, halved

1 tablespoon red curry paste

1 tablespoon fish sauce

1 tablespoon honey

4 cups low sodium chicken broth

1 1/2 cups light coconut milk

2 cups cooked and shredded boneless skinless chicken breasts

3 tablespoons lime juice

INSTRUCTIONS

1. Heat a large pot over medium heat. Add the oil to the pot and

swirl to coat. Add in the red bell pepper, shallots, mushrooms, ginger and lemongrass. Cook for 3 minutes, stirring occasionally.
2. Add in the garlic, snow peas and red curry paste and cook for another minute. Add in the chicken broth, fish sauce, and honey; bring to a simmer. Reduce heat to low and simmer for 10 minutes.
3. Add the coconut milk and chicken to the pot and cook for another 2-3 minutes or until heated through. Stir in the lime juice and discard the lemongrass. Serve the soup topped with cilantro, scallions and thinly sliced Thai chiles.

Detox Chicken Soup

yield: 6 SERVINGS

prep time: 10 MINUTES

cook time: 20 MINUTES

total time: 30 MINUTES

INGREDIENTS:

2 tablespoons olive oil, divided

1 pound boneless, skinless chicken breasts, cut into 1-inch chunks

Kosher salt and freshly ground black pepper

1 onion, diced

2 carrots, peeled and diced

2 celery ribs, diced

4 cloves garlic, minced

16 ounces cremini mushrooms, thinly sliced

1/2 teaspoon dried thyme

1/2 teaspoon dried oregano

8 cups chicken stock

2 bay leaves

1/2 cup uncooked orzo pasta

1 sprig fresh rosemary

1 bunch kale, stems removed and leaves chopped

1 (15-ounce) can cannellini beans, drained and rinsed

Juice of 1 lemon

2 tablespoons chopped fresh parsley leaves

DIRECTIONS:

1. Heat 1 tablespoon olive oil in a large stockpot or Dutch oven over medium heat. Season chicken with salt and pepper, to taste. Add chicken to the stockpot and cook until golden, about 2-3 minutes; set aside.
2. Add remaining 1 tablespoon oil to the stockpot. Add onion, carrots and celery. Cook, stirring occasionally, until tender, about 3-4 minutes.
3. Add garlic and mushrooms, and cook, stirring occasionally, until tender and browned, about 5-6 minutes. Stir in thyme and oregano until fragrant, about 1 minute.
4. Whisk in chicken stock and bay leaves; bring to a boil. Stir in orzo, rosemary and chicken; reduce heat and simmer until orzo is tender, about 10-12 minutes.
5. Stir in kale and cannellini beans until the kale has wilted, about 3-4 minutes. Stir in lemon juice and parsley; season with salt and pepper, to taste.
6. Serve immediately.

Mediterranean Kale, Cannellini And Farro Stew

Servings: 6

Prep Time 15 minutes

Cook Time 45 minutes

Total Time 1 hour

INGREDIENTS

2 Tbsp olive oil

1 cup carrots diced (about 2 medium)

1 cup chopped yellow onion (1 small)

1 cup chopped celery (about 2)

4 cloves garlic , minced

5 cups low-sodium vegetable broth

1 (14.5 oz) can diced tomatoes

1 cup farro , rinsed

1 tsp dried oregano

1 bay leaf

Salt , to taste

1/2 cup slightly packed parsley sprigs (stems included)

4 cups slightly packed chopped kale , thick ribs removed

1 (15 oz) can cannellini beans, drained and rinsed

1 Tbsp fresh lemon juice

1/2 cup Feta cheese , crumbled, for serving

INSTRUCTIONS

1. Heat oil in a large pot over medium-high heat.
2. Add carrots, onion and celery and saute 3 minutes. Add garlic and saute 30 seconds longer.
3. Stir in vegetable broth, tomatoes, farro, oregano, bay leaf and season with salt to taste.
4. Add parsley in a mound to soup and bring soup to a boil. Reduce heat just below medium.
5. Cover and simmer 20 minutes. Then remove parsley, stir in kale and cook 10 - 15 minutes longer until both farro and kale are tender.
6. Adding in cannellini beans and heat through, about 1 minute.
7. Remove bay leaf, stir in lemon juice and add additional vegetable broth or some water to thin soup as desired (the farro will absorb more liquid as the soup rests).
8. Serve warm topping each serving with feta cheese.

Jalapeño Lime Chicken Soup

Prep Time: 30 mins

Cook Time: 1 hour

Yield: 6

INGREDIENTS

2 tablespoons olive oil

2 jalapeños, ribs and seeds removed, minced

half of a red onion, minced

4 cups water

1 teaspoon salt (more as needed)

1 pound boneless skinless chicken breasts or thighs

2 14-ounce cans white beans, drained (canellini or great northern)

1 16-ounce jar salsa verde

juice of 2 limes

fresh cilantro, sour cream, and shredded cheese for serving

INSTRUCTIONS

1. In a soup pot over medium heat, saute the onion and jalapeno with the olive oil until soft and fragrant.
2. Add the water and salt. Bring to a boil. Add the raw chicken breasts. Cover and cook for 5-10 minutes. Remove from heat, but leave the lid on so that the chicken continues cooking for another 20 minutes. Remove the chicken breasts, set aside to cool.
3. Add the white beans and salsa to the pot. Simmer for 30

minutes over medium heat.

4. Shred the chicken and add it back to the pot.
5. Just before serving, squeeze the juice of one lime into the pot. Cut the remaining lime into wedges for serving. Add the salt; taste and adjust as needed. Serve with fresh cilantro, sour cream, and shredded cheese.

Cabbage Soup

Prep Time: 15 minutes

Cook Time: 25 minutes

Total Time: 40 minutes

Servings: 6

INGREDIENTS

1 tablespoon olive oil

3/4 cup onion diced

1 cup carrots peeled, halved and sliced

1/2 cup celery sliced

2 teaspoons minced garlic

1 red bell pepper cut into 1/2 inch pieces, seeds and core removed

1 green bell pepper cut into 1/2 inch pieces, seeds and core removed

3 cups cabbage coarsely chopped

15 ounce can diced tomatoes do not drain

1 teaspoon dried Italian seasoning

salt and pepper to taste

6 cups chicken broth

3/4 cup green beans cut into 1/2 inch pieces

2 tablespoons parsley chopped

INSTRUCTIONS

1. Heat the olive oil in a large pot over medium heat. Add the onion, carrot and celery and cook for 4-5 minutes.
2. Add the garlic to the pot and cook for 30 seconds. Add the red and green peppers, cabbage, tomatoes, Italian seasoning, salt, pepper and chicken broth to the pot.
3. Bring to a simmer; cook for 10-15 minutes or until vegetables are tender.
4. Add the green beans and cook for an additional 5 minutes or until tender. Sprinkle with parsley, then serve.

Pesto Chicken Minestrone

YIELDS: 8 servings

TOTAL TIME: 1 hour 0 mins

INGREDIENTS

1 head garlic

3 tbsp. olive oil, divided

1 small onion, chopped

8 c. chicken stock

1 1/4 lb. boneless, -skinless chicken breast

1 large piece Parmesan cheese rind

1 (15.5-ounce) can dark red kidney beans, rinsed

2 large carrots, sliced

1/4 tsp. crushed red pepper

1 (9-ounce) package fresh four-cheese tortellini

1 bunch curly kale, stems discarded and leaves torn

2 tbsp. prepared pesto, plus more for serving

Kosher salt

Freshly ground black pepper

DIRECTIONS

1. Preheat oven to 400°F. Cut off pointed end of garlic, exposing cloves. Place on a piece of aluminum foil and drizzle with 1

tablespoon oil; wrap tightly. Bake until soft, 35 to 40 minutes; let cool. Squeeze pulp from garlic and mash into a paste; reserve.

2. Meanwhile, heat remaining 2 tablespoons oil in a large pot or Dutch oven over medium-high heat. Add onion and cook, stirring occasionally, until golden brown, 4 to 6 minutes. Add chicken stock, chicken breast, and Parmesan rind. Bring to a boil. Reduce heat to low and simmer, covered, until chicken is cooked through, 25 to 30 minutes. Remove chicken and shred with two forks; return to pot.

3. Stir in beans, carrots, red pepper, and 2 tablespoons reserved mashed garlic. Simmer, covered, 15 minutes. Uncover and stir in tortellini. Cook, uncovered, stirring occasionally, 4 to 6 minutes. Stir in kale and cook until pasta is cooked through and kale is tender, 2 to 4 minutes. Remove from heat and discard Parmesan rind. Stir in 2 tablespoons pesto. Season with salt and pepper. Serve warm with additional pesto.

Savory Pumpkin Soup With Spice Shake

YIELDS: 8 servings

TOTAL TIME: 1 hour 5 mins

INGREDIENTS

Soup

1/4 c. olive oil

1 sweet onion, chopped

1 red bell pepper, seeded and chopped

Kosher salt and freshly ground black pepper

2 cloves garlic, chopped

1 tbsp. chili powder

2 tsp. dried oregano

2 (15-ounce) cans pure pumpkin puree

2 qt. vegetable broth

3 tbsp. fresh lime juice

Spice Shake, for serving

Spice Shake

2 tbsp. whole cumin seeds

2 tbsp. whole fennel seeds

2 tbsp. whole coriander seeds

1 c. toasted pepitas

2 tsp. crushed red pepper

1 tsp. kosher salt

DIRECTIONS

1. Make the soup: Heat oil in a large saucepan over medium-high heat. Add onion and bell pepper. Season with salt and pepper. Cook, stirring occasionally, until onion is soft, 8 to 10 minutes. Add garlic, chili powder, and oregano. Cook, stirring, until fragrant, about 30 seconds.
2. Add pumpkin puree and broth. Cook, stirring occasionally, until slightly thickened, 25 to 30 minutes. Working in batches, puree soup in a blender until smooth. Season with salt and pepper. Stir in lime juice just before serving. Serve with Spice Shake alongside.
3. Make the Spice Shake: Cook 2 tbsp. each whole cumin seeds, whole fennel seeds, and whole coriander seeds in a small skillet over low heat, stirring, until fragrant, 1 to 2 minutes; transfer to a bowl. Add 1 cup toasted pepitas, 2 teaspoons crushed red pepper, and 1 teaspoon kosher salt. Makes 1 2/3 cups.

Crock Pot Chicken Tortilla Soup

PREP TIME: 5 MINUTES

COOK TIME: 3 HOURS

TOTAL TIME: 3 HOURS 5 MINUTES

SERVINGS: 6

INGREDIENTS

1 onion chopped

2 cloves garlic minced

1 tablespoon olive oil

3 cups low sodium chicken broth

1 8 ounce can tomato sauce

1 14.5 ounce can fire roasted diced tomatoes (or regular if you prefer less spicy)

1 4.5 ounce can Old El Paso green chiles

1/4 cup chopped cilantro

4 cups cooked and shredded chicken or rotisserie chicken

1 1 ounce packed Old El Paso Taco Seasoning

1 11 ounce can steamed corn, drained and rinsed

For the tortilla strips

2 cups canola oil

2 8 " Old El Paso Burrito Tortillas

1 tablespoon Old El Paso Taco Seasoning

Optional garnishes

cilantro Old El Paso sliced Jalapenos, low fat sour cream, low fat shredded cheese

INSTRUCTIONS

1. Heat oil over medium/high heat in a medium skillet. Add onion and garlic and cook until translucent, about 3 minutes. I like mine to be a bit under-sauteed, to keep a bit of their crunch.
2. Once sauteed, add the onion and garlic to a slow cooker over high heat. Add in all other ingredients except for tortillas and garnishes. Stir to combine.
3. Heat on high, covered, for 2-3 hours, or on low for 4-5 hours.
4. Before serving, prepare the tortilla crisps:
5. In a small saucepan, heat the canola oil over medium/high heat.
6. Using a pizza cutter, cut each tortilla into 1/2 inch strips.
7. Cook the strips in batches, about 2-4 minutes or until browned.
8. Using a slotted spoon, remove the strips and allow to drain on a paper towel.
9. While strips are still hot and before they've dried, sprinkle with taco seasoning and salt to taste. Allow to dry completely.
10. When ready to serve the soup, serve garnished with extra cilantro, low fat sour cream, jalapenos, and tortilla strips. Or any of your favorite toppings!

Chicken Vegetable Soup

Prep Time: 20 minutes

Cook Time: 35 minutes

Total Time: 55 minutes

Servings: 6

INGREDIENTS

1 tablespoon butter

1/2 cup onion finely diced

2 carrots peeled, halved lengthwise and sliced

2 stalks celery thinly sliced

2 teaspoons minced garlic

3 cups cooked chicken shredded or cubed

salt and pepper to taste

15 ounce can diced tomatoes do not drain

8 ounce can tomato sauce

1 teaspoon Italian seasoning

6 cups chicken broth

1 large Russet potato peeled and cut into 1/2 inch cubes

1/2 cup frozen corn

1/2 cup diced green beans fresh or frozen

2 tablespoons chopped fresh parsley

INSTRUCTIONS

1. Melt the butter in a large pot over medium high heat. Add the onion, carrots and celery to the pot.
2. Cook for 5-6 minutes or until softened. Add the garlic and cook for 30 seconds more. Season with salt and pepper to taste.
3. Add the chicken, tomatoes, tomato sauce, Italian seasoning, chicken broth and potato to the pot; bring to a simmer.
4. Cook for 20-25 minutes or until potatoes are tender. Taste and add salt and pepper as desired.
5. Stir in the corn and green beans and cook for 5 minutes more. Sprinkle with parsley and serve.

Lemon Chicken And Cauliflower Rice Soup

yield: 4 SERVINGS

prep time: 10 MINUTES

cook time: 15 MINUTES

total time: 25 MINUTES

INGREDIENTS

1 teaspoon olive oil

1 cup diced yellow onion

32 ounces low sodium chicken broth

12 ounces cauliflower, riced (I used a bag of frozen defrosted cauliflower rice)

2 tablespoons fresh chopped dill, divided

Zest of a lemon

1/3 cup fresh lemon juice

4 teaspoons cornstarch or arrowroot powder

2 eggs, whisked

1 pound cooked boneless skinless chicken breasts, shredded

INSTRUCTIONS

1. Add the olive oil to a large pot over medium-high heat. When the oil is hot add in the diced onion and sauté 2-3 minutes. Add in 1 tablespoon of the fresh chopped dill, lemon zest and the chicken broth. Season with salt and pepper and bring to a boil.
2. Add in the cauliflower rice and simmer until it's tender, about

6-8 minutes.

3. In a small bowl whisk the arrowroot powder (or cornstarch) and lemon juice together until the arrowroot is dissolved.
4. Whisk the eggs into the lemon juice mixture then slowly ladle in about 1-2 cups of the broth whisking the entire time so that the eggs don't curdle. Once the mixture comes to temperature whisk it back into the soup pot. Continue to stir the mixture until it thickens slightly, about 5 minutes.
5. Add in the shredded chicken and remaining tablespoon of chopped dill. Taste for seasoning and adjust as needed. Serve the soup topped with thin lemon slices and extra dill if desired.

Vegetable Beef Soup

Prep: 15 mins

Cook: 2 hrs 50 mins

Total: 3 hrs 5 mins

Serves: 8

INGREDIENTS

2 lbs stewing beef or chuck roast, cut in 1 inch cubes

8 cups water

3 tbsp olive oil

1 large onion chopped

2 carrots chopped

2 stalks celery chopped

1 tsp salt or to taste

1/2 tsp pepper or to taste

3 tbsp tomato paste

14.5 oz diced tomatoes (1 can)

1 beef bouillon or 2 tbsp vegeta

1 cup cauliflower florets

1 small zucchini chopped

1/4 cup lemon juice freshly squeezed

1 large egg beaten

1/4 cup parsley chopped

INSTRUCTIONS

1. Cook the beef: Add the beef and water to a large pot. Bring to a

boil over medium high heat. Once the broth starts to boil, remove all the impurities from the top. If you don't, you'll get a cloudy dark soup, instead of a nice clear broth.

2. Reduce to a simmer, cover the pot and cook for about 1 1/2 to 2 hours. You need to cook this until the beef is tender. Once the beef is done remove it from the broth, keep the broth.

3. Saute veggies: In a large Dutch oven, heat the olive oil over medium high heat. Add the onion, carrots, celery and saute until tender, about 5 minutes. Season with salt and pepper. Stir in the tomato paste and the diced tomatoes. Add the beef bouillon or vegeta.

4. Add beef, cauliflower and simmer: Add the cauliflower and cooked beef to the pot. Add the beef broth (from cooking the beef) and stir. Bring to a boil, then turn down the heat to a simmer and cook for about 30 minutes.

5. Add Zucchini, lemon juice and cook for 10 more minutes: Stir in the zucchini and lemon juice. Cook for another 10 minutes or until the zucchini is tender.

6. Add egg: Pour the egg mixture into the soup and quickly stir. You will notice the soup thickening up a bit, the egg will cook instantly.

7. Garnish and serve: Garnish with parsley and serve with sour cream and pickled hot peppers.

30 Minute Pesto Chicken, Kale + White Bean Soup

Prep Time: 10 minutes

Cook Time: 20 minutes

Total Time: 30 minutes

Yield: 4-6 servings

INGREDIENTS

1/2 cup plus 1 tablespoon extra virgin olive oil

2 medium carrots, scrubbed and thinly sliced

2 stalks celery, thinly sliced

1 large yellow or Spanish onion, diced

2 cloves garlic, minced, plus 1-2 cloves for pesto*

2 quarts chicken stock, homemade or boxed

2 cans white beans (cannelloni or great northern), drained and rinsed

1 lb boneless skinless chicken breasts (about 2 medium)

1 bunch kale (I used Tuscan/lacinato but any variety works), tough stems removed and cut or torn into pieces

3 tablespoons pine nuts (not toasted)

3 packed cups fresh basil

1/2 cup extra virgin olive oil, plus more for serving

1/4 cup grated parmesan cheese, plus more for serving

juice of 1 lemon

INSTRUCTIONS

1. Pour 1 tablespoon olive oil in a large pot over medium heat. Add the carrots, celery and onion, then cook, stirring occasionally, until softened, about 5 minutes. Add the garlic and cook for 2 minutes more.
2. Add the chicken stock and white beans, stir, then submerge the chicken breasts. Cover, bring to a boil, then reduce the heat and simmer until the chicken is cooked through, about 10 minutes.
3. While the chicken cooks, make the pesto. Add 1 large or 2 smaller cloves garlic to the bowl of a food processor. Pulse until coarsely chopped, then add the pine nuts and basil. Continue pulsing as you slowly stream in the olive oil. Add the parmesan cheese and pulse a few more times until everything is well combined. Season to taste with salt and pepper.
4. Remove the chicken breasts and let cool, then use two forks to shred into bite sized pieces. Add the chicken back to the pot along with the kale, stir, then cover and cook just a few minutes more until the kale is wilted.
5. Stir in the pesto and lemon juice, then ladle into bowls. Sprinkle with more grated parmesan and a drizzle of olive oil, then serve it piping hot.

NOTES

*Use 1 large clove to make the pesto or 2 if smaller.

Lentil Soup

Servings: 6

Prep Time: 10 minutes

Cook Time: 1 hour

Total Time: 1 hour 10 minutes

INGREDIENTS

2 Tbsp olive oil

1 1/2 cups diced carrots (3 medium)

1 1/2 cups diced yellow onions (1 medium)

1 1/2 Tbsp minced garlic (4 cloves)

4 (14.5 oz) cans vegetable broth

2 (14.5 oz) cans diced tomatoes

1 1/4 cups dried brown lentils , rinsed and picked over

1 1/2 tsp dried basil

1/2 tsp dried oregano

1/2 tsp dried thyme

Salt and freshly ground black pepper

1 1/2 cups diced zucchini (1 medium)

2 cups packed chopped kale or spinach

1 Tbsp fresh lemon juice

Parmesan cheese , for serving (optional)

INSTRUCTIONS

1. Heat olive oil in a large pot over medium-high heat.
2. Add carrots and onions and saute 2 minutes then add garlic and

saute 2 minutes longer.
3. Pour in vegetable broth and tomatoes. Add in lentils, basil, oregano, thyme and season with salt and pepper to taste.
4. Bring to a boil then reduce heat to medium-low, cover and simmer 35 minutes, stirring occasionally.
5. Add in zucchini and kale and simmer 10 minutes longer, if using spinach wait to add it until the last 2 minutes.
6. Stir in lemon juice and add up to 1 cup of water to thin as needed (as the soup rests the lentils soak up more of the broth).
7. Serve warm with parmesan cheese if desired.

NOTES

- Stick with brown or green lentils or adjust the cooking time. Red lentils cook in over half the cooking time of brown and green.
- If you don't have have the dried herbs listed here, you could also substitute 1 Tbsp dried Italian seasoning instead of basil, oregano and thyme.
- If you are out of vegetable broth, chicken broth will work too.
- Don't skip the lemon. Even though it's a small amount it adds a nice hint of brightness.

Curried Cauliflower Soup

Prep Time: 15 mins

Cook Time: 45 mins

Total Time: 1 hour

Yield: 4 bowls

INGREDIENTS

1 large head of cauliflower, broken into small florets, stems chopped

Up to 4 tablespoons melted coconut oil or olive oil, divided

1 medium yellow onion, diced

2 to 3 tablespoons Thai red curry paste* (depending on preferred

spice level, I love spicy so I'd use 3!)

½ teaspoon lemon zest

½ cup unoaked white wine (like Sauvignon Blanc or Pinot Grigio)**

1 ½ cups vegetable broth or stock

1 can (14 ounces) light coconut milk

½ teaspoon sugar

1 to 3 teaspoons rice vinegar

Salt and freshly ground black pepper

¼ cup chopped green onions or chives

1 tablespoon chopped fresh basil

Thinly sliced jalapeño, Serrano or birds-eye peppers (optional, not shown)

INSTRUCTIONS

1. Preheat oven to 400 degrees Fahrenheit. Toss the cauliflower with enough coconut oil to lightly coat it (up to 3 tablespoons). Spread the cauliflower in a single layer on a large baking sheet and roast until the tips of the cauliflower are golden brown, about 25 to 30 minutes.

2. In a Dutch oven or large, heavy-bottomed pot over medium heat, warm 1 tablespoon of the coconut oil until shimmering. Add the onion and a dash of salt and cook, stirring occasionally, until the onion is turning translucent, about 3 minutes. Add the curry paste and lemon zest and stir to incorporate. Raise the heat to medium-high, add the wine, and cook, stirring frequently, until most of the wine has evaporated.
3. Add all of the roasted cauliflower stems and half of the florets to the pot. Add the vegetable broth, coconut milk and sugar. Bring the mixture to a gentle simmer, stirring occasionally. Continue simmering for 5 to 10 more minutes to meld the flavors, reducing heat as necessary to maintain a gentle simmer. Remove the pot from the heat.
4. Let the soup cool for a few minutes, then carefully use an immersion blender to blend until smooth. (Or transfer the soup in small batches to a blender, blending until each batch is smooth. Don't ever fill your blender past the maximum fill line, and beware of the steam escaping from the lid.)
5. Stir in 1 teaspoon vinegar and salt and pepper, to taste. If the soup needs more acidity, stir in 1 to 2 additional teaspoons of vinegar, to taste. Ladle the soup into 4 bowls. Top each with ¼ of the cauliflower florets, a sprinkle of basil and chives and hot peppers (if using).

Superfood Quinoa Soup

yield: 8 SERVINGS

prep time: 15 MINUTES

cook time: 20 MINUTES

total time: 35 MINUTES

INGREDIENTS:

1 tablespoon olive oil

3 cloves garlic, minced

1 red onion, diced

3 carrots, peeled and diced

2 stalks celery, diced

1/2 teaspoon dried thyme

1/2 teaspoon dried oregano

4 cups vegetable stock

2 bay leaves

1 cup quinoa

1 bunch kale, stems removed and leaves chopped

8 ounces broccoli florets

2 cups shredded red cabbage

Juice of 1 lemon

Kosher salt and freshly ground black pepper, to taste

2 tablespoons chopped fresh parsley leaves

DIRECTIONS:

1. Heat olive oil in a large stockpot or Dutch oven over medium heat.
2. Add garlic, onion, carrots and celery. Cook, stirring occasionally, until tender, about 3-4 minutes. Stir in thyme and oregano until fragrant, about 1 minute.
3. Whisk in vegetable stock, bay leaves and 2 cups water; bring to a boil. Stir in quinoa; reduce heat and simmer until quinoa is tender, about 12-15 minutes.
4. Stir in kale, broccoli and cabbage; simmer, stirring occasionally, until kale is tender, about 5 minutes. Stir in lemon juice; season with salt and pepper, to taste.
5. Serve immediately, garnished with parsley, if desired.

Paleo Turkey Meatball Zoodle Soup

Prep Time: 10 minutes

Cook Time: 25 minutes

Total Time: 35 minutes

Servings: 8 servings

INGREDIENTS

meatballs:

1 lb ground turkey not too lean

1 large egg

1/4 cup blanched almond flour

1/2 tsp fine grain sea salt

1 tsp onion powder

1 tsp garlic powder

1 tsp poultry seasoning blend

Large pinch crushed red pepper

1 Tbsp avocado oil or olive oil

soup:

2 Tbsp avocado oil or olive oil

1 med onion diced

4 cloves garlic minced

3 cups kale roughly chopped

6 cups chicken bone broth or no-sugar added chicken broth

1 bay leaf

2 tsp minced fresh sage

2 tsp minced fresh rosemary

1 lb zucchini noodles or about 3 small-med zucchini, spiralized

Sea salt and black pepper to taste

Fresh minced parsley for garnish

INSTRUCTIONS

for the meatballs:

1. In a large bowl, combine all meatball ingredients and mix well with slightly wet hands (to prevent sticking).
2. Heat a large skillet* over med/med-hi heat and add 1 Tbsp oil. With wet hands, for the mixture into small meatballs about 1" diameter and carefully add to the hot skillet to brown. It helps to wet your hands once they start getting sticky for easy rolling. Turn meatballs a couple of times to brown, then remove from heat and set aside.

for the soup:

1. Heat a large stock pot or dutch oven over medium heat and add the 2 Tbsp oil. Add the onion and cook until soft. Add the garlic and cook another 30 seconds, then add kale and stir to coat, sprinkle with sea salt, and sauté another 2 minutes until softened.

2. Add in the broth, bay leaf, and herbs and heat to boiling, lower heat to a simmer, then add meatballs back in to cook through - about 10 mins.
3. Add in zucchini noodles at the 6-8 minute mark so as not to overcook them. Season with sea salt and pepper to taste, and garnish with fresh parsley to serve. Enjoy!

NOTES

- Alternatively, you can brown the meatballs in the same dutch oven that you're using for the soup. I chose a large skillet to get them all in there in one batch.

15 Minute Tomato Basil Soup With Pesto

Prep Time: 5 mins

Cook Time: 10 mins

Total Time: 15 mins

Servings: 6 servings (approximately 1 cup per serving)

INGREDIENTS

1 Tbsp olive oil

1 yellow onion, peeled and diced

2 cloves garlic, minced

2 (15 oz each) cans no salt added fire-roasted diced tomatoes, undrained

1 cup fat-free reduced sodium chicken broth

1/4 tsp kosher salt

pinch black pepper

1/4 cup fresh basil, chopped

1 tsp balsamic vinegar

1/4 cup half and half

2 Tbsp basil pesto (pre-made)

INSTRUCTIONS

1. In a soup pot or large saucepan, add olive oil and heat over MED/MED-HIGH heat. Add diced onion and cook 4 minutes, until softened and slightly browned. Add garlic and

cook about a minute.

2. Add cans of tomatoes, broth, salt and pepper and stir to combine. Bring to a boil, then turn off heat to low and stir in chopped basil and vinegar.
3. Use an immersion blender to blend until smooth (or until your desired consistency). Alternatively, add soup to blender (removing the center piece to allow steam to escape, and covering the opening with a kitchen towel), and blend until smooth. Transfer soup from blender back to the soup pot.
4. Stir in half and half and let heat through. Ladle into serving bowls and swirl in approximately 1 tsp of pesto and an optional tsp of half and half and garnish with additional basil if desired.

Italian Wedding Soup

prep time: 15 MINUTES

cook time: 20 MINUTES

total time: 35 MINUTES

servings: 12

INGREDIENTS

For the meatballs:

2 pounds ground turkey sausage, or chicken sausage

1 cup gluten free bread crumbs

1 large egg

5 tablespoons milk

For the soup:

1 tablespoon olive oil

1 onion, peeled and chopped

3 cloves garlic, minced

1 cup sliced carrots

1 cup sliced celery

3 tablespoons fresh chopped dill

2 tablespoon fresh chopped parsley

12 cups chicken broth

1 ½ cups gluten free pasta (use any small shape)

1 cup fresh baby spinach, packed

1 tablespoon lemon juice

¼ - ½ teaspoon crushed red pepper

½ cup shaved parmesan cheese

INSTRUCTIONS

1. For the meatballs: In a large bowl mix the ground turkey sausage, gluten free bread crumbs, egg, and milk. Mix by hand until the mixture is very smooth.
2. Place a large 6-8 quart soup pot over medium heat. Add the oil, chopped onion, garlic, carrots, and celery to the pot. Sauté for 5 minutes, to soften the vegetables.
3. Add the dill, parsley, and chicken broth. Bring to a simmer.
4. While the soup is heating, roll the meat into small tight 1 inch balls. Once the soup starts to simmer, add in the meatballs, 3-5 at a time, stirring so they don't stick to the bottom.
5. After all the meatballs are in the soup, simmer an additional 5 minutes. Then stir in the gluten free pasta, spinach, lemon juice, and crushed red pepper. Simmer the pasta 6-8 minutes, or according to the package instructions.
6. Taste, salt and pepper as needed. Serve warm with a sprinkling of parmesan cheese.

NOTES

- Gluten Free pasta does not hold up in liquid very long. It will need to be eaten right away. If not gluten free, use standard bread crumbs and pasta, so the soup can be enjoyed as leftovers.

Spinach And White Bean Soup

yield: 6 SERVINGS

prep time: 10 MINUTES

cook time: 20 MINUTES

total time: 30 MINUTES

INGREDIENTS:

1 tablespoon olive oil

3 cloves garlic, minced

1 onion, diced

1/2 teaspoon dried thyme

1/2 teaspoon dried basil

4 cups vegetable stock

2 bay leaves

1 cup uncooked orzo pasta

2 cups baby spinach

1 (15-ounce) can cannellini beans, drained and rinsed

Juice of 1 lemon

2 tablespoons chopped fresh parsley leaves

Kosher salt and freshly ground black pepper, to taste

DIRECTIONS:

1. Heat olive oil in a large stockpot or Dutch oven over medium heat. Add garlic and onion, and cook, stirring frequently, until onions have become translucent, about 2-3 minutes. Stir in thyme and basil until fragrant, about 1 minute.

2. Whisk in vegetable stock, bay leaves and 1 cup water; bring to a boil. Stir in orzo; reduce heat and simmer until orzo is tender, about 10-12 minutes.
3. Stir in spinach and cannellini beans until the spinach has wilted, about 2 minutes. Stir in lemon juice and parsley; season with salt and pepper, to taste.
4. Serve immediately.

Summer Vegetable, Chicken, and Gnocchi Soup

YIELDS: 4 - 6 servings

INGREDIENTS

1 c. chopped sweet onion

2 chopped garlic cloves

2 tbsp. butter

2 zucchini, sliced small

2 tsp. fresh dill

6 c. chicken stock

2 c. rotisserie chicken

1 (16-oz.) package gnocchi

1 1/2 c. halved green beans

1/2 (5-oz.) bag (about 4 cups) baby spinach

2 tbsp. fresh lemon juice

Extra fresh dill, for serving

DIRECTIONS

1. Cook sweet onion and garlic cloves in butter in a large pot over medium-high heat until translucent, 4 to 6 minutes. Stir in zucchini and fresh dill; cook 30 seconds. Stir in chicken stock, cover, and simmer for 3 minutes.
2. Stir in rotisserie chicken, gnocchi, and green beans. Cover and simmer until beans are crisp-tender, 3 to 4 minutes. Stir in baby spinach and lemon juice.
3. Simmer until spinach is wilted, 1 to 2 minutes. Season with kosher salt and black pepper. Serve topped with fresh dill.

Snap Pea-and-Lettuce Soup

YIELDS: 4 servings

TOTAL TIME: 0 hours 30 mins

INGREDIENTS

2 leeks, sliced (white and green parts only)

1/4 c. butter

8 c. chicken stock

2 Yukon Gold potatoes, peeled

1 lb. snap peas, trimmed

2 romaine hearts, chopped

3 tbsp. fresh tarragon

1/2 c. Buttermilk

kosher salt, to taste

Freshly ground black pepper, to taste

DIRECTIONS

1. Cook leeks in butter in a medium pot until tender. Add chicken stock and Yukon Gold potatoes; simmer until potatoes are tender.
2. Add snap peas and romaine hearts; simmer until bright green.
3. Puree (in batches) along with fresh tarragon until smooth; strain.
4. Stir in buttermilk. Season with salt and freshly ground black pepper.